Jataka Tales

Interesting Stories of
Gautam Buddha's Past Lives

Retold By
Clifford Sawhney

UNICORN BOOKS

Publishers
UNICORN BOOKS

F-2/16, Ansari Road, Daryaganj, New Delhi-110002
☎ 23275434, 23262683, 23262783 • *Fax:* 011-23257790
E-mail: unicornbooks@vsnl.com • Website: www.unicornbooks.in

Distributors
Pustak Mahal®, Delhi
J-3/16, Daryaganj, New Delhi-110002
☎ 23276539, 23272783, 23272784 • Fax: 011-23260518
E-mail: info@pustakmahal.com • Website: www.pustakmahal.com

Sales Centres
- 10-B, Netaji Subhash Marg, Daryaganj, New Delhi-110002
  ☎ 23268292, 23268293, 23279900 • *Fax:* 011-23280567
  E-mail: salespmahal@airtelmail.in
           rapidexdelhi@indiatimes.com
- 6686, Khari Baoli, Delhi-110006
  ☎ 23944314, 23911979
- **Bengaluru:** ☎ 22234025 • *Telefax:* 22240209
  E-mail: pustak@airtelmail.in • pustak@sancharnet.in
- **Mumbai:** ☎ 22010941
  E-mail: rapidex@bom5.vsnl.net.in
- **Patna:** ☎ 3294193 • *Telefax:* 0612-2302719
  E-mail: rapidexptn@rediffmail.com
- **Hyderabad:** *Telefax:* 040-24737290
  E-mail: pustakmahalhyd@yahoo.co.in

© **Copyright: Unicorn Books**

ISBN 978-81-7806-088-3

Edition: 2010

Printed at : Param Offsetters, Okhla, New Delhi-110020

Introduction

Jataka Tales were told by Gautam Buddha (563 BC–483 BC) himself to stress the importance of moral values and explain concepts like rebirth. A total of 547 in number, the tales revolve around the past lives of the Buddha, sometimes as an animal and at other times as a human. Originally passed by word of mouth from generation to generation, these tales of wisdom and morals were first written in Pali around 300 BC and later translated into other languages.

Many of the tales are set in Benares (now Varanasi) and have animal characters who speak and act much like humans, teaching the values of self-sacrifice, honesty, morality, perseverance etc. Especially when the joint family system is breaking up and both parents could be working, the Jataka Tales are particularly relevant in our modern times, since children need proper guidance to lead stable lives and succeed professionally when they are adults.

Contents

The Shovel Wise Man

Once upon a time, the Buddha was born into a family of vegetable gardeners. After he grew up he cleared a patch of land with his shovel. He grew herbs, pumpkins, melons, cucumbers and other vegetables. These he sold to earn a decent living.

The shovel was his one and only possession in the whole world. He carried it with him everywhere. Some people thought he carried it in the same way a forest monk carries his walking staff. So he became known as the 'Shovel Wise Man'.

One day he thought, "What good does it do me to live the ordinary everyday life of a gardener? I will give up this life and go meditate in the forest. Then I will be peaceful and happy."

So the Shovel Wise Man hid his one possession, the shovel, and became a forest meditator.

*****

Before long, he started thinking about his only possession, the shovel. He was so attached to this shovel that he couldn't get it out of his mind, no matter how hard he tried! Trying to meditate seemed useless, so he gave it up. He returned to the shovel and his ordinary life as a vegetable gardener.

Lo and behold, in a little while the Shovel Wise Man again gave up his everyday life, hid his shovel and became a forest meditator. Again he could not get the shovel out of his mind, and returned to being a gardener. All in all, this happened six times!

The next time the Shovel Wise Man gave up his forest meditation, he finally realised it was because of his old worn-out shovel that he had gone back and forth seven times! So he decided to throw it away, once and for all, in a deep river. Then he would return to the forest for good.

He took his shovel down to the riverbank. He thought, "Let me not see where this shovel enters the water. Otherwise it may tempt me again to give up my quest." So he closed his eyes, swung the shovel in a circle over his head thrice, and let it fly into the middle of the river.

Realising that he would never be able to find the shovel again, he shouted, just like a lion roars, "I have conquered! I have conquered! I have conquered!"

*****

It just so happened that the King of Benares was riding by at that very moment. He was returning from putting down a revolt in a border village. He had bathed in the river, and had just seated himself on his magnificent royal elephant. He was riding back to Benares in a victory procession.

When he heard the triumphant shouts of the Enlightened Being, he told his ministers, "Listen! Who is shouting, just like a lion roars, 'I have conquered'? Whom has he conquered? Bring that man to me!"

When they brought the Shovel Wise Man to him, the king said, "I am a conqueror because I have won a battle. You say that you have conquered. Whom did you conquer?"

The Shovel Wise Man replied, "Your Lordship, even if you conquer a hundred thousand armies, they are meaningless victories if you still have unwholesome thoughts and desires in your own mind! By conquering the craving in my mind, I know I have won the battle against unwholesome thoughts."

As he spoke, he concentrated on the water in the river, then on the idea of water itself, and reached a high mental state. In a sitting position he rose into the air. He preached these words of Truth to the king: "Defeating an enemy who returns to fight you again and again is no real victory. But if you defeat the unwholesomeness in your own mind, no one can take that true victory from you!"

While the king was listening to these words, all unwholesome thoughts left his mind. It occurred to him to give up the ordinary world and seek real peace and happiness. He asked, "Where are you going now, wise one?"

The Shovel Wise Man answered, "I am going to the Himalayas, O King, to practise meditation."

The king said, "Please take me with you. I too wish to give up the common worldly life."

Lo and behold, as the king turned northward with the Shovel Wise Man, so did the entire army and all the royal ministers and attendants.

*****

Soon the news reached the people of Benares that the king and all those with him were leaving the ordinary world and following the Shovel Wise Man to the Himalayas. Then all the people in the entire city of Benares followed them towards the northern mountains. Benares was empty!

This great migration of people came to the attention of the god Sakka, King of the Heavens. Never had he seen so many giving up worldly power. He ordered the architect of the gods to build a dwelling place in the Himalayan forests for all these people.

When they arrived in the Himalayas, the Shovel Wise Man was the first to announce that he had given up the ordinary world for good. Then all those with him did the same. Never was so much worldly power given up at the same time.

The Shovel Wise Man developed what holy men call the 'Four Heavenly States of Mind'. First, loving kindness and tender affection for all. Second, feeling sympathy and pity for all those who suffer. Third, feeling happiness for all those who are joyful. And fourth, balance and calm, even in the face of difficulties or troubles. He taught the others advanced meditation. With great effort they all gained high mental states, leading to rebirth in heaven worlds.

■ ■

The Golden Swan

Many years ago, there lived a holy Brahmin. He and his wife had three sweet daughters. Although very poor, the family was very happy. The Brahmin worked hard and looked after his family well. The children never ever felt they were poor.

One day, the Brahmin fell very sick. The village doctor tried his best to treat the Brahmin. But he kept growing weaker and weaker everyday. A few weeks later, the Brahmin died in his sleep. His wife was filled with grief. "My lord, now that you are gone, who will look after us? What will happen to our three little daughters?" she cried and beat her chest in grief.

Seeing this, all the neighbours rushed to the Brahmin's wife. "Do not worry, sister," they said. "Nothing will happen to you and your small daughters. We will help you in every way we can." With this promise from the neighbours, the Brahmin's widow felt better.

From that day, the neighbours always prepared some extra food. Each day, the Brahmin widow would visit a different neighbour and take some food or grains from them. In this way, their needs were met. The neighbours also kept aside old clothes. These were then given to the Brahmin's widow and her daughters.

Some time later, the Brahmin took birth again as a swan. He lived in a beautiful lake surrounded by hills. The calm blue waters of the lake made life very pleasant. Yet, the swan was very restless. He still remembered his life as a Brahmin and always thought of his family.

"I wonder how my wife and three little girls must be living," he worried. "Life must be very hard for them after I died. I must visit them and find out. Perhaps they need my help."

With these thoughts in mind, the swan flew to his old village. When he reached there, he felt very sad. His wife was going from door to door, collecting food and clothes. "My family has to beg for their living," the swan moaned. "I must do something."

He quickly flew to the roof of their hut. One of his daughters saw him. By then his wife had returned from her daily rounds. "Look Mummy! A swan with golden feathers is on the roof," the daughter said, excited.

"Let us catch the golden swan," chirped another daughter.

The Brahmin's widow ran after the swan with a cloth in hand. "Don't catch me!" the swan cried out. "I am your husband, now reborn as a swan. I am here to help you."

The Brahmin's widow was amazed on hearing this. "I will give you one golden feather everyday," the swan continued. "You can sell this daily. With the money, you can run the house easily. You will never need to stretch your hand before anybody."

Having said this, the swan shed a golden feather. The Brahmin's widow quickly picked up the golden feather. She then sold this in the market. With the money, she bought food and clothes.

From that day onwards, the Brahmin's family was very happy. They bought the best food grains and fruits. The girls wore the nicest clothes. The Brahmin woman bought the best jewellery. They even hired some servants to do all the housework. The neighbours wondered how the Brahmin widow had suddenly become rich. But no one knew their secret.

*****

One day, however, a strange thought entered the Brahmin widow's head. She told her daughters, "Suppose the swan stops coming to our house one day? He is a free bird. He could do what he wants. What will happen to us after this? Our only means of living would be taken away. What is the use of taking just one feather everyday? It is better if we pluck all the feathers at once. This way we will get all the riches at once. We will never have to worry about anything again."

But the daughters were against this idea. "No mother! Please do not do such a thing. The swan has been helping us daily. Do not think of hurting him," the girls pleaded.

However, the Brahmin widow refused to listen. That day, when the swan came, she grabbed him by the neck. Quickly, she began plucking his golden feathers one by one.

"No!" the swan honked in alarm. "You cannot pluck all my feathers at one time. They will be useless. Please listen to me."

Blinded by greed, the Brahmin's widow refused to listen. Within a short while, the swan lay helpless on the ground. All his feathers had been plucked. Now, he simply couldn't fly.

The Brahmin's wife quickly gathered all the feathers. "I will not have to wait for a silly swan everyday," she laughed in glee. But as she picked up the feathers, she was horrified. The golden feathers had suddenly turned white!

"What is this!" cried the Brahmin widow. "All the feathers have turned white. These are useless. You have cheated me."

"I had warned you," replied the Brahmin. "But you did not listen. Now you must pay the price."

The Brahmin's widow was very angry on hearing this. She quickly flung the swan into their courtyard. The bird lay there hurt for some time.

*****

For the next few days, the swan simply kept running about. Without feathers, he couldn't fly. After two weeks, his feathers had slowly regrown. But these were now white. "Let me go away from here," the swan told himself. "It is no use living with a wicked woman. She is totally thankless, despite all I have done for her."

So saying, the swan flew away. He never ever returned to his family again. As for the Brahmin's family, all their money was soon used up. Their servants also left them because they were not paid. Very sadly, the proud widow began begging for food once again. Now, the neighbours also did not wish to help them. Due to her greed, there was no golden swan to help them too. Soon, they became poor once again. All because the Brahmin widow's greed had blinded her.

■ ■

The Meditating Holy Man

In one of his many rebirths, the Buddha was born into a rich and powerful family. When he grew up he became dissatisfied with simply chasing the ordinary pleasures of the world. So he gave up his former lifestyle, including his wealth and position. He went to the foothills of the Himalayas and became a holy man.

It so happened that one day he ran out of salt. So he decided to go and collect alms. He came upon a caravan and went with it part of the way on its journey. In the evening they stopped and made camp.

The holy man began walking at the foot of a big tree nearby. He concentrated until he had entered a high mental state. He remained in that state throughout the night, while he continued to walk around the tree.

Meanwhile, 100 bandits had surrounded the campsite. They waited until after dinner, when all had settled down for the night. But before they could attack, they noticed the holy man. They told each other, "That man must be on guard for security. If he sees us, he'll warn the rest. So let's wait until he falls asleep, and then rob and loot!"

What the bandits didn't know was the holy man was so deep in meditation that he didn't notice them at all - or anything else for that matter! So they kept waiting for him to fall asleep. And he just kept walking and walking and walking - until the light of dawn finally began to appear. Only then did he stop meditating.

Having had no chance to rob the caravan, the bandits threw down their weapons in frustration. They shouted, "Hey, you people in the caravan! If your security guard hadn't stayed up all night, walking under that tree, we would have robbed you all! You should reward him well!" With that they left in search of another group to rob.

When it became light the people in the caravan saw the clubs and stones left behind by the bandits. Trembling with fear, they went over to the holy man. They greeted him respectfully and asked if he had seen the bandits. "Yes, this morning I did," he said.

"Weren't you scared?" they asked.

"No," said the holy man. "The sight of bandits is only frightening to the rich. But I'm not a rich man. I own nothing of any value to robbers. So why should I be afraid of them? I have no anxiety

17

in a village, and no fear in the forest. Possessing only loving kindness and compassion, I follow the straight path leading to Truth."

In this manner he preached the way of fearlessness to the lucky people of the caravan. His words made them feel peaceful, and they honoured him.

■■

The Holy Fish

Once upon a time, the Buddha was born as a fish in a pond in northern India. There were many kinds of fish, big and small, living in the pond with the Bodhisattva.

There came a time when there was severe drought, as the rainy season did not come as usual. The crops of farmers died, and many ponds, lakes and rivers dried up. The fish and turtles dug down and buried themselves in the mud, frantically trying to keep wet and save themselves. All this pleased the crows. They simply stuck their beaks down into the mud, pulled up the frightened little fish, and feasted on them.

The suffering of pain and death by the other fish filled the Buddha-fish with sadness. He felt pity and compassion for his fellow fish. He realised that he was the only one who could save them. But it would take a miracle.

The truth was that he had remained innocent by never taking the life of anyone. He was determined to use the power of this wholesome truth to make rain fall from the sky, and release his relatives from their misery and death. He pulled himself up from under the black mud. He was a big fish, and as black from the mud as polished wood. He opened his eyes, which sparkled like rubies, looked up to the sky, and called on the rain god Pajjunna. He exclaimed, "Oh my friend Pajjunna, god of rain, I am suffering for the sake of my relatives. Why do you withhold rain from me, who is perfectly wholesome, and make me suffer in sympathy with all these fish?

"I was born among fish, amongst whom it is customary to eat other fish – even our own kind, like cannibals! But since I was born, I myself have never eaten any fish, even one as tiny as a grain of rice. In fact, I have never taken life from anyone. The truthfulness of this innocence of mine gives me the right to tell you: Make the rains fall! Relieve the suffering of my relatives!"

The Buddha-fish said this the way one gives orders to a servant. And he continued, commanding the mighty rain god Pajjunna: "Make rain fall from the thunderclouds! Do not allow the crows their hidden treasures! Let the crows feel the sorrow of their unwholesome actions. At the same time release me from my sorrow, for having lived in perfect wholesomeness."

After only a short pause, the sky opened up with heavy showers of rain, relieving many from the fear of death – fish, turtles and even humans. And when the great Buddha-fish who had worked this miracle eventually died, he was reborn as he deserved.

■■

The Gang of Drunkards

Once upon a time, when Brahmadutta was king, the Buddha was born in a wealthy family. He soon became the richest man in Benares.

There also happened to be a gang of drunkards who roamed the streets of Benares. All they ever thought about was finding ways to get alcohol, which they thought they couldn't live without.

One day, when they had run out of money as usual, they came up with a plan to rob the richest man in Benares. But they didn't realise that he was the reborn Bodhisattva, so he wouldn't be so easy to fool!

They decided to make a *Special Santra* – a drink of liquor with a sleeping drug secretly added to it. Their plan was to get the rich man to drink the *Special Santra*. Then when he fell asleep they would rob all his money, jewellery, and even the costly clothes he wore. So they set up a temporary little roadside bar. They put their last remaining liquor into a bottle, and mixed some strong sleeping pills.

Later the rich man came by on his way to the palace. One of the drunkards called out to him, "Honourable sir, why not start your day right - by having a drink with us? And the first one is on the house!" Then he poured a glass of the drugged liquor.

But the rich man did not drink any form of alcohol. Nevertheless, he wondered why these drunkards were being so generous with their favourite drink. It just wasn't in their nature to do so.

He realised it must be some kind of trick. So he decided to teach them a lesson. He said, "It would be an insult to appear before the king in a drunken state, or with even the slightest smell of liquor on my breath. But please be so kind as to wait for me here. I'll see you again when I return from the palace."

The drunkards were disappointed. They would not be able to drink again as soon as they wanted. But they decided to be patient and wait.

*****

Later that day the rich man came back to the little roadside bar. The drunkards were getting desperate for a drink. They called him over, "Honourable sir, why not celebrate your visit to the king? Have a drink of this fine liquor. Remember, the first one is free!"

But the rich man just kept looking at the liquor bottle and glass. He said, "I don't trust you. That glass of liquor is exactly as it was this morning. If it were as good as you say it is, you would have tasted some yourselves by now. In fact, you couldn't help but drink it all! I'm no fool. You must have added another drug to the alcohol."

The richest man in Benares went on his way unharmed. And the gang of drunkards went back to their plotting and scheming.

■ ■

The Bowl of Gold

There was once a merchant of Seri who sold brass and tin-ware. He went from town to town, in company with another man, who also sold brass and tin-ware. This second man was greedy, getting all he could for nothing, and giving as little as he could for what he bought.

When they went into a town, they divided the streets between them. Each man went up and down the streets he had chosen, calling: "Tin-ware for sale! Brass for sale!" Each merchant was only allowed to enter the other's streets when the first merchant had moved out. People came out to their doorsteps, and bought, or traded, with them.

In one house there lived a poor old woman and her granddaughter. The family had once been rich, but now the only thing they had left was a golden bowl. The grandmother did not know it was a golden bowl, but she had kept this because her husband used to eat out of it in the old days. It stood on a shelf among the other pots and pans, and was not often used.

The greedy merchant passed this house, calling, "Buy my water-jars! Buy my pans!"

The granddaughter said: "Oh, Grandmother, do buy something for me!"

"My dear," said the old woman, "we are too poor to buy anything. I have not anything to trade, even."

"Grandmother, see what the merchant will give for the old bowl. We do not use that, and perhaps he will take it and give us something we want for it."

The old woman called the merchant and showed him the bowl, saying, "Will you take this, sir, and give the little girl here something for it?"

The greedy man took the bowl and scratched its side with a needle. Thus he found that it was a golden bowl. He hoped he could get it for nothing, so he said: "What is this worth? Not even a half-penny." He threw the bowl on the ground, and went away.

*****

By and by the other merchant passed the house. It was agreed that either merchant might go through any street the other had left. He called: "Buy my water-jars! Buy my tin-ware! Buy my brass!"

The little girl heard him, and begged her grandmother to see what he would give for the bowl.

26

"My child," said the grandmother, "the merchant who was just here threw the bowl on the ground and went away. I have nothing else to offer in trade."

"But, Grandmother," said the girl, "that was a rude man. This one looks pleasant. Ask him. Perhaps he'll give some little tin dish."

"Call him, then, and show it to him," said the old woman.

As soon as the merchant took the bowl in his hands, he knew it was of gold. He said: "All that I have here is not worth so much as this bowl. It is a golden bowl. I am not rich enough to buy it."

"But, sir, a merchant who passed here moments ago, threw it on the ground saying it was not worth half-penny, and he went away," said the grandmother. "It was worth nothing to him. If you value it, take it, giving the little girl some dish she likes for it."

But the merchant would not have it so. He gave the woman all the money he had, and all his wares. "Give me only eight pennies," he said.

So he took the pennies, and left. Going quickly to the river, he paid the boatman the eight pennies to take him across the river to the city.

*****

Soon the greedy merchant went back to the house where he had seen the golden bowl, and said: "Bring that bowl to me, and I will give you something for it."

"No," said the grandmother. "You said the bowl was worthless, but another merchant has paid a great price for it, and taken it away."

Then the greedy merchant was angry, crying out, "Through this other man I have lost a small fortune. That bowl was of gold."

He ran down to the riverside and, seeing the other merchant in the boat out in the river, he called: "Hello, boatman! Stop your boat!"

But the man in the boat said: "Don't stop!" So he reached the city on the other side of the river, and lived well for a time on the money the bowl had fetched him.

■■

The Smart Deer

A big, strong and handsome deer once lived in a forest near Varanasi. Daily, he wandered through the forest searching for food. One day, he came across a forest patch with trees having the tastiest berries. The grass here too was very juicy and tasty.

From that day onwards, the deer stopped roaming the forest. He only visited this place daily to fill his stomach. One day, a hunter noticed this deer. He soon grew curious because of the animal's habit of visiting a certain part of the forest only.

So the hunter kept a watch on the animal. One day, he quietly followed the deer. Soon, the hunter found the forest patch with the juiciest berry trees. The hunter now thought, "This deer has the biggest antlers I have ever seen. If I can catch and kill him, I could sell his antlers for a lot of money."

*****

The very next day, the hunter went and hid up a berry tree. He knew the deer would come there as usual. The hunter was very right. The deer went there as he did daily.

But the deer was also very smart. He always kept a close watch of his surroundings. He knew the danger from tigers, leopards and human hunters. As the deer looked all around, he noticed human footprints on the jungle floor. Immediately, his ears stood up. "Perhaps there is some human hunter waiting to catch me," he thought. "So I better be very careful."

The deer then began eating the grass that was some distance away from the berry trees. The hunter waited for more than an hour. Slowly, he grew tired of waiting. "Why is the deer not coming closer to eat the berries?" he wondered. "Let me throw some berries down to tempt him."

So thinking, the hunter threw some berries at the deer. The deer's suspicions were quickly confirmed. He looked up amongst the leaves. However, due to the thick branches, he could not spot the hunter. The deer therefore decided to fool the hunter and clear his doubts.

"My dear talking tree," the deer said, "why are you not speaking to me today? And why is it that you are throwing the berries at me? Everyday you simply drop berries at my feet very gently. Speak up, else I will go away and never return."

The hunter was confused. "Perhaps this is a magic tree that speaks to the deer everyday," he told himself. "If I keep silent, the deer will go away. And I will lose my only chance to kill it."

So without thinking twice, the hunter called out: "Please do not go away, deer! Here, I am dropping a few berries at your feet."

As the hunter said this, he bent forward to drop the berries. The deer now noticed the human hunter. Without a backward glance, he quickly ran away. Too late, the hunter realised he had been fooled by a handsome but smart deer.

■ ■

The Bulbul Vs the Hornbill

In days long gone by, the hornbill ruled the bird kingdom. He was a very bad king, though. Big or small, all the birds were very scared of him. Even for small mistakes, he would beat up the other birds. Nobody could ever tell what would make the hornbill angry on some days.

One day when the birds could no longer take his unjust rule, they held a meeting. All the birds gathered quietly under a shady banyan tree. The nasty hornbill was not told about the meeting. "We must decide on selecting a new king," spoke up the timid sparrow. The once-chirpy sparrow had received the most beatings from the hornbill. So she overcame her fear and spoke: "If we do not do so, the hornbill may soon begin to kill us when he is angry."

"The sparrow is right," piped the tiny kingfisher. She too had faced the hornbill's anger many times.

The myna, the parrot, the lapwing, the bulbul, the crow, the owl, the koel, the pigeon and many other birds shook their heads in agreement.

"But who should be made king?" asked the koel.

"It has to be somebody strong enough to handle the hornbill's bullying ways," insisted the crow.

The other birds nodded once again. But the koel disagreed: "Let us not exchange one bad king for another. The king should be soft and kind-hearted."

So many names went back and forth. Finally, all agreed that the bulbul seemed the best person for this role. The bulbul was hardworking and never bothered anyone. So the bulbul's name was cleared.

"There is one more thing," the pigeon cooed. "Who will tell the hornbill he is no more our king?"

"Whoever does so will be beaten black and blue," warned the parrot.

The wise owl now opened her beak: "I have an idea!"

All the birds quickly turned towards the owl hopefully. "Here is my plan. And the woodpecker will have to help me in this," the owl said.

She then told the other birds about her plan. "Wonderful!" "That's a good idea!" "It will definitely work." "The hornbill will never realise our game." The birds had only positive comments to make about the owl's plan. The woodpecker was happy that he could play an important role.

****

33

Later that day, the owl met the hornbill. "Your Lordship," the owl bowed. "All the birds feel that every year you must prove you are fit to rule us once more."

"What do you mean?" the hornbill narrowed his eyes in anger.

"It is a very simple test, Your Majesty," the owl replied. "You will have to break the thick branch of a tree. If you do so, you will be king for another year. If not, other birds will have a chance. The bird that breaks the branch wins."

The hornbill gave a loud laugh. He knew his strength and was sure that he would win against any other bird. "Okay," he announced. "Just show me which branch has to be broken. I will do it in a jiffy."

The wily owl then took the hornbill to a neem tree. Here, the owl pointed to a thick branch. The confident hornbill hopped onto the branch and proceeded to strike it with his strong beak. For the next hour, the hornbill delivered one blow after another. Although part of the branch was weakened, it showed no signs of breaking. Two hours later, the hornbill stopped, dead tired.

"The hornbill's turn is now up," declared the owl. "The bulbul will now take his turn." So saying, the owl flew near an extremely thick branch. "The bulbul will try to break this branch."

On hearing this, the hornbill laughed heartily. There was no way a tiny bird like the bulbul could break such a thick branch. "The bulbul will not even be able to shake this branch," the hornbill laughed, "leave alone break it."

The clever owl hid a smile. And the bulbul bravely flew up to the branch. Then, with all her strength, the bulbul landed heavily on the branch. In a second, the branch creaked and cracked.

few seconds later, the branch had broken and fallen to the forest floor.

The hornbill was left speechless. The owl grinned from ear to ear. All the birds rose and chirped in one voice: "Long live the bulbul! Long live our new king!" The bulbul bowed all around.

As the birds patted the bulbul, the hornbill flew away quietly. She was ashamed of how a tiny bulbul had beaten her. Unknown to the hornbill, the owl had played a trick. The night before, the owl had whispered something to the woodpecker. Throughout the night, the woodpecker then kept pecking the thick branch at a point where leaves covered it. When the branch was just one peck away from breaking, the woodpecker stopped. The next day, when the bulbul landed on it heavily, the branch simply fell away. This was all because of the woodpecker's hard work.

Thanks to the owl's trick, the hornbill was defeated. And the birds now had a new and just ruler and lived happily ever since.

■■

The Mosquito and
the Senseless Son

Once upon a time when Brahmadutta was reigning in Benares, the Bodhisattva earned his living as a trader. In those days, a number of carpenters dwelt at a border village in Kasi. It so happened that one of them, a bald grey-haired man, was cutting some wood with his head shining like a copper plate. Just then, a mosquito settled on his bald head and stung him with its thorn-like sting.

The carpenter told his son, who was seated nearby, "My boy, there's a mosquito stinging me on the head. Please drive it away."

"Hold still then, father," said the son. "One blow will kill it."

At that very time the Bodhisattva had reached this village and was sitting in the carpenter's shop.

"Rid me of it!" cried the father.

"All right, father," answered the son, who was behind the old man's back. Then, raising a sharp axe high to kill only the mosquito, he split his father's head into two. The old man died on the spot.

The Bodhisattva was an eyewitness to the whole scene. He said to himself: "Better than such a friend is an enemy with sense, whom fear of men's vengeance will deter from killing a man."

■ ■

The Timid Hare and the World's End

Once upon a time when Brahmadutta reigned in Benares, the Bodhisattva took birth as a young lion. When he was fully grown, he lived in a thick forest. At this time there was a grove of palms mixed with vilva trees near the Western Ocean.

A certain hare lived here beneath a palm sapling, at the foot of a vilva tree. One day after feeding, this hare came and lay down beneath the young palm tree. And the thought struck him, "If this earth should be destroyed, what would become of me?"

And at this very moment a ripe vilva fruit fell on a palm leaf. At the sound of it, the hare thought, "This solid earth is collapsing," and getting up, he fled without so much as looking behind him. Another hare saw him running away, as if frightened to death, and asked the cause of his panic flight.

"Pray, don't ask me," he said.

The other hare cried, "Pray, sir, what is it?" and kept running after him.

Then the hare stopped a moment and without looking back said, "The earth here is breaking up."

At this, the second hare ran after the other. And so, first one and then another hare caught sight of him running, and joined in the chase till one hundred thousand hares all took flight together. Soon, a deer, a boar, a buffalo, a wild ox, a rhinoceros, a tiger, a lion, and an elephant saw them. And when they asked what it was all about and were told that the earth was breaking up, they too took flight. So slowly, this group of animals extended miles across.

When the Bodhisattva saw this headlong flight of the animals, and heard that the cause was the earth coming to an end, he thought, "The earth is nowhere coming to an end. Surely it must be some sound that was misunderstood by them. And if I don't make a great effort, they will all perish. I must save their lives."

So with the speed of a lion, he got before them to the foot of a mountain and, lion-like, roared thrice. They were terribly frightened by the lion, and stopping in their flight all huddled together. The lion went in amongst them and asked why they were running away.

"The earth is collapsing," they answered.

"Who saw it collapsing?" he asked.

"The elephants know all about it," they replied.

He asked the elephants. "We don't know," they said, "the lions know."

But the lions said, "We don't know, the tigers know."

The tigers said, "The rhinoceroses know."

The rhinoceroses said, "The wild oxen know."

The wild oxen, "The buffaloes."

The buffaloes, "The boars."

The boars, "The deer."

The deer said, "We don't know, the hares know."

When the hares were questioned, they pointed to one particular hare and said, "This one told us."

So the Bodhisattva asked, "Is it true, sir, that the earth is breaking up?"

"Yes, sir, I saw it," said the hare.

"Where," he asked, "were you living, when you saw it?"

"Near the ocean, sir, in a grove of palms mixed with vilva trees. For as I was lying beneath the shade of a palm sapling at the foot of a vilva tree, methought, 'If this earth should break up, where shall I go?' And at that very moment I heard the sound of the earth breaking up, and I fled."

Thought the lion, "A ripe vilva fruit evidently must have fallen on a palm leaf and made a 'thud', and this hare jumped to the conclusion that the earth was coming to an end, and ran away. I will find out the exact truth about it."

So he reassured the herd of animals, and said, "I will take the hare and go and find out exactly whether the earth is coming to an end or not, in the place pointed out by him. Until I return, stay here."

Then he placed the hare on his back, sprang forward with the speed of a lion, and putting the hare down in the palm grove, said, "Come, show us the place you meant."

"I dare not, my lord," said the hare.

"Come, don't be afraid," said the lion.

The hare, not venturing to go near the vilva tree, stood afar and cried, "Yonder, sir, is the place of dreadful sound," and so saying, he repeated the first stanza:

From the spot where I did dwell
Issued forth a fearful "thud";
What it was I could not tell,
Nor what caused it understood.

After hearing what the hare said, the lion went to the foot of the vilva tree. Here he saw the spot where the hare had been lying beneath the shade of the palm tree, and the ripe vilva fruit that fell on the palm leaf. Having carefully ascertained that the earth had not broken up, he placed the hare on his back and with the speed of a lion soon came again to the herd of beasts.

Then he told them the whole story, and said, "Don't be afraid." And having thus reassured the herd of beasts, he let them go.

Truly, had it not been for the Bodhisattva at that time, all the beasts would have rushed into the sea and died. It was thanks to the Bodhisattva that they escaped death.

■ ■

The Tortoise Who Wouldn't Leave Home

When Brahmadutta was reigning in Benares, the Bodhisattva was born in a village as a potter's son. With a wife and family to support, he plied the potter's trade.

At that time there lay a great natural lake close by the great river of Benares. When there was much water, the river and the lake were one. But when the water level was low, they grew apart. Now fish and tortoises knew by instinct when the year would be rainy and when there would be drought.

One year, the fish and tortoises living in the lake knew there would be drought. So, when the lake and river were one, they swam out of the lake and into the river. But one tortoise refused to go into the river. Said he, "I was born here and I grew up here. Here is my parents' home. I cannot leave it at any cost!"

*****

Later, in the hot season, all the water dried up. So the tortoise dug a hole and buried himself, just where the Bodhisattva used to come for clay. One day, the Bodhisattva came for some clay. With a big spade he dug down, until he cracked the tortoise's shell, turning him out on the ground as though he were a large piece of clay. In his agony the creature cried, "Here I am dying, all because I was too fond of my home to leave it!"

So telling the Bodhisattva, he died. The Bodhisattva picked him up and collected all the villagers. He then told them: "Look at this tortoise. When the other fish and tortoises went into the great river, he was too fond of his home to go with them. So he buried himself in the place where I get my clay. Then as I was digging for clay, I broke his shell with my big spade, and turned him over on the ground in the belief that he was a large lump of clay. Then he told me what he had done, lamented his fate in two verses of poetry, and expired.

"So you see he came to his end because he was too fond of his home. Take care not to be like this tortoise. Don't say to yourselves, 'I have sight, I have hearing, I have smell, I have taste, I have touch, I have a son, I have a daughter, I have numbers of men and maids for my service, I have precious gold.' Do not cling to these things with craving and desire."

■■

43

The Strong Ox

Long ago, a man owned a very strong Ox. The owner was so proud of his Ox that he boasted to every man he met about how strong his Ox was.

One day the owner went into a village. There, he told the men: "I will pay a thousand pieces of silver if my strong Ox cannot draw a line of one hundred wagons."

The men laughed, and said: "Very well; bring your Ox, and we will tie a hundred wagons in a line and see your Ox draw them along."

So the man brought his Ox into the village. A crowd gathered to see the sight. The hundred carts were in line, and the strong Ox was yoked to the first wagon.

Then the owner whipped his Ox, and said: "Get up, you wretch! Get along, you rascal!"

But the Ox had never been talked to in this manner, and he stood still. Neither the blows nor the hard names could make him move.

At last the poor man paid up, and went home sadly. There he threw himself on his bed and cried: "Why did that strong Ox act so? Many a time he has moved heavier loads easily. Why did he shame me before all those people?"

At last he got up and went about his work.

*****

When he went to feed the Ox that night, the Ox turned to him and said: "Why did you whip me today? You never whipped me before. Why did you call me 'wretch' and 'rascal'? You never called me hard names before."

Then the man said: "I will never treat you badly again. I am sorry I whipped you and called you names. I will never do so anymore. Forgive me."

"Very well," said the Ox. "Tomorrow I will go into the village and draw the one hundred carts for you. You have always been a kind master until today. Tomorrow you shall gain what you lost."

*****

The next morning the owner fed the Ox well, and hung a garland of flowers about his neck. When they went into the village the men laughed at the man again.

They said: "Did you come back to lose more money?"

"Today I will pay a fine of two thousand pieces of silver if my Ox is not strong enough to pull the one hundred carts," said the owner.

So again the carts were placed in a line, and the Ox was yoked to the first. A crowd came to watch again. The owner said: "Good Ox, show how strong you are! You fine creature!" And he patted his neck and stroked his sides.

At once the Ox pulled with all his strength. The carts moved on until the last cart stood where the first had been.

Then the crowd clapped, and they paid back the fine the man had lost, saying: "Your Ox is the strongest Ox we ever saw."

And the Ox and the man went home, happy.

■ ■

The Chain of Interdependence

In a deep forest clearing, the trees were having a pre-dawn discussion. "Animals come and rest in our shade but they leave a mess behind," said the Jamun. "The smell on some days is unbearable!"

"They show no concern for us because we're silent," said the Sal. "But I've had enough! I've made up my mind to drive away any animal that comes here!"

"That may not be a wise thing to do," said the Peepal, the oldest and biggest tree there. The Bodhisattva had taken birth as a Peepal tree this time. "The animals are a nuisance, I agree, but they serve a useful purpose. We are all inter-dependent – trees, animals, men..."

"I'm sorry," interrupted the Sal. "I've great respect for your views but in this matter I will not listen to anyone. I won't allow animals here anymore!"

True to his word when a leopard came to rest in the shade later that day, the Sal began to shake violently from side to side. The leopard, frightened out of his wits, jumped up and ran away. The Sal drove away all the animals that came to the clearing that day and in the days that followed. In course of time the animals stopped coming to that part of the forest.

The Sal became a great hero to the younger trees in the neighbourhood. Even some of the older ones began bowing to him when the Peepal was not looking.

*****

Then one day two woodcutters came to the clearing. "Men!" gasped the Sal. "Why have they come here? They've never come here before."

"If they've never come here before it was because they were afraid of the animals," said the Peepal. "Now the absence of the leopard and the tiger has made them bold."

The Sal began to tremble with fear and with good reason. It was the first tree the woodcutters chopped down. Then one by one all the other trees also fell to their axes.

■■

Monks in the Pleasure Garden

Once upon a time, the Bodhisattva was reborn as a high-class rich man. He gave up his wealth and easy life in the ordinary world. He went to the Himalayan forests and lived as a homeless holy man. By practising meditation, he developed his mental powers, enjoyed great inner happiness and peace of mind: Soon, he had 500 pupils.

In a certain year, when the rainy season was beginning, the pupils told their teacher, "O wise master, we would like to go to the places where most people live. We would like to get some salt and other seasonings and bring them back here."

The teacher said, "You have my permission. It would be healthy for you to do so, and return when the rainy season is over. But I will stay here and meditate by myself." They knelt down and paid their farewell respects.

The 500 pupils went to Benares and began living in the royal pleasure garden. The next day they collected alms in the villages outside the city gates. They received generous gifts of food. On the following day they went inside the city. People gladly gave them food.

After a few days, people told the king, "O Lord, 500 forest monks have come from the Himalayas to live in luxuries. They control their senses and are known to be very good indeed."

Hearing such good reports, the king went to meet them. He knelt down and paid his respects. He invited them to stay in the garden during the entire four months of the rainy season. They accepted, and from then on were given their food in the king's palace.

Before long a certain holiday took place. It was celebrated by drinking alcohol, which the people thought would bring good luck. The King of Benares thought, "Good wine is not usually available to monks who live simply in the forests. I will treat them to some as a special gift." So he gave the 500 forest monks a large quantity of the best tasting wine.

The monks were not at all accustomed to alcohol. They drank the king's wine and walked back to the garden. By the time they got there, they were completely drunk. Some of them began dancing, while others sang songs. Usually they put away their bowls and other things neatly. But this time they just left everything lying around all over the place. Soon they all passed out into a drunken sleep.

When they had slept off their drunkenness, they awoke and saw the messy condition they'd left everything in. They were sad and told each other, "We have done a bad thing, which is not proper for holy men like us." Their embarrassment and shame made them weep with regret. They said, "We have done these unwholesome things only because we are far away from our holy teacher."

That very moment the 500 forest monks left the pleasure garden and returned to the Himalayas. When they arrived they put away their bowls and other belongings neatly, as was their custom. Then they went to their beloved master and greeted him respectfully.

He asked them, "How are you, my children? Did you find enough food and lodging in the city? were you happy and united?"

They replied, "Venerable master, we were happy and united. But we drank what we were not supposed to drink. We lost all our senses and self-control. We danced and sang like silly monkeys. It's fortunate we didn't turn into monkeys! We drank wine, we danced, we sang, and in the end we cried from shame."

The kind teacher said, "It is easy for things like this to happen to pupils who have no teacher to guide them. Learn from this and do not do such things in the future."

■■

The Wise Tree Spirit

Once upon a time, as happens to all beings, the King of the Tree Spirits died. King Sakka, ruler of the Heavens, appointed a new King of the Tree Spirits. As his first official act, the new king sent out a notice that every tree spirit should choose a tree to live in. Likewise it was stated that every tree was to be pleased with its resident spirit.

It so happened that a very wise tree spirit was the leader of a large clan. He advised his clan members not to live in freestanding trees. Instead it would be safer to live in the forest trees near him. The wise tree spirits settled down in the forest trees with their leader.

But there were also some foolish and arrogant tree spirits. They said to each other, "Why should we live in this crowd? Let us go to the villages, towns and cities inhabited by human beings. Tree spirits who live there receive the best offerings. And they are even worshipped by superstitious people living in those places. What a life we will have!"

So they went to the villages, towns and cities, and moved into the big freestanding trees looked after by people.

*****

Then one day a big storm came up. The wind blew strong and hard. The big heavy trees with old stiff branches did not do well in the storm. Branches fell down, trunks broke in two, and some were even uprooted. But the trees in the forest, which were intertwined with each other, were able to bend and support each other in the mighty wind. They did not break or fall!

The tree spirits in the villages, towns and cities had their homes destroyed. They gathered up their children and returned to the forest. They complained to the wise leader about their misfortune in the big lonely trees in the land of men.

He simply said, "This is what happens to arrogant ones who ignore wise advice and go off by themselves."

■■

53

The Poisonous Tree

Once upon a time there lived a caravan leader. He went from country to country selling various good. His caravans usually had at least 500 bullock carts.

On one of these trips his path led through a very thick forest. Before entering it, he called together all the members of the caravan. He warned them, "My friends, when you go through this forest be careful to avoid the poisonous trees, poisonous fruits, poisonous leaves, poisonous flowers and even poisonous honeycombs.

"Therefore, whatever you have not eaten before - whether a fruit, leaf, flower or anything else - must not be eaten without asking me first."

They all said respectfully, "Yes sir."

*****

There was a village in the forest. Just outside the village stood a tree called a 'whatnot tree'. Its trunk, branches, leaves, flowers and fruits look very similar to a mango tree. Even the colour, shape, smell and taste were almost exactly the same as a mango tree. But unlike a mango, the whatnot fruit was a deadly poison!

Some went ahead of the caravan and came upon the whatnot tree. They were all hungry, and the whatnot fruits looked like delicious ripe mangoes. Some began eating the fruit immediately, without thinking at all. They devoured them before anyone could say a word.

Others remembered the leader's warning, but they thought this was just a different variety of mango tree. They thought they were lucky to find ripe mangoes right next to a village. So they decided to eat some of the fruit before they were all gone.

There were also some who were wise, unlike the rest. They decided it would be safer to obey the warning of the caravan leader. Although they didn't know it, he just happened to be the Buddha.

*****

When the leader arrived at the tree, the ones who had been careful and not eaten asked, "Sir, what is this tree? Is it safe to eat these fruits?"

After investigating thoughtfully, he replied, "No, no! This may look like a mango tree, but it isn't. It is a poisonous whatnot tree. Don't even touch it!"

The ones who had already eaten the whatnot fruit were terrified. The caravan leader asked them to force themselves to vomit as soon as possible. They did this, and then were given four sweet foods to eat - raisins, cane sugar paste, sweet yoghurt and bee's honey. In this way their taste buds were refreshed after throwing up the poisonous whatnot fruit.

*****

Unfortunately, the greediest and most foolish ones could not be saved. They were the ones who had begun eating the poisonous fruit immediately, without thinking at all. It was too late for them. The poison had already started taking effect, and it killed them.

In the past, when caravans had come to the whatnot tree, people had eaten its poisonous fruits and died in their sleep during the night. The next morning the local villagers had come to the campsite. They had grabbed the dead bodies by the legs, dragged them to a secret hiding place, and buried them. Then they took away all the merchandise and bullock carts of the caravan.

They expected to do the same thing this time. At dawn the next morning the villagers ran towards the whatnot tree. They said to each other, "The bullocks will be mine!" "I want the carts and wagons!" "I will take the loads of merchandise!"

But when they got to the whatnot tree they saw that most of the people in the caravan were alive and well. In surprise, they asked them, "How did you know this was not a mango tree?"

They answered, "We did not know, but our leader had warned us ahead of time, and when he saw it, he knew."

Then the villagers asked the caravan leader, "O wise one, how did you know this was not a mango tree?"

He replied, "I knew it for two reasons. First, this tree is easy to climb. And second, it is right next to a village. If the fruits on such a tree remained unpicked, they could not be safe to eat!"

Everyone was amazed that such lifesaving wisdom was based on simple common sense. The caravan continued on its way safely.

■■

The Large-hearted Monkey

In a forest mountain glade, by the side of the river Ganges, there lived about eight thousand monkeys along with their giant monkey king. And by the side of the clear gushing water stood a tall shady tree bearing big beautiful juicy golden mangoes.

All the monkeys just loved these mangoes and ate them almost as soon as they had ripened. This was a very good thing, as their wise king had warned them not to let a single juicy fruit fall into the river. Because if the current carried even one of these fruits down the river to the land where men lived, they would surely come in search of this delicious fruit. Then the peace in the land of monkeys would be destroyed.

It so happened that a branch of this tree hung low over the river and a mango that was hidden behind an ant's nest ripened and fell off without anyone noticing. It was taken down south by the rapid flow of the river and reached the city of Benares.

*****

One fine morning when King Brahmadutta of Benares was bathing in the river between two nets, a couple of fishermen found a bright golden fruit caught in the mesh of the net. Excited, they took it to show the king.

The king examined the fruit carefully and asked where it had come from and what it was called. The fishermen did not know much about it but guessed that it must have flowed down the river from the valleys of the far-flung Himalayas. So the king asked them to cut the mango and tasted a slice. It was simply delicious. He shared the rest of it with his ministers and queen who loved its divine flavour.

A few days passed, but the king could not get this strange fruit out of his mind. He could not work, rest or sleep for want of some more. Finally, he could bear it no longer and set sail in search of this strange fruit. He organised a fleet of rafts and sailed up the river accompanied by his men and a few fishermen.

Many days and nights went by and they passed many valleys until they finally came to the one where the mango tree stood. The goal reached, the king was delighted and began enjoying the mangoes to his heart's content.

*****

Finally, that night, the king lay down to sleep under the mango tree while his faithful soldiers stood guard. Fires were lit on either side for protection against wild animals.

In the middle of the night when the guards had dozed off to sleep, the monkeys came and finished off all the mangoes that were left on the tree. The king awoke with all the noise and ordered his guards to shoot the monkeys so that they could feast on monkey flesh along with the mangoes.

On hearing this, the monkeys trembled with fear and escaped to inform their king. They told him what had happened and he promised to save them. But for that he had to come up with a plan.

So he climbed up the tree and swung across the river with the help of a branch. He found a bamboo shoot, which he measured and cut carefully, and then tied one end of it around his waist. The other end he tied around a tree trunk. He had decided to leap back to the mango tree and help the rest of the monkeys cross over the bridge he had made with the help of the bamboo shoot.

But alas... he had not taken into account the portion that he had tied around his waist. So when the monkey king sprang back into the mango grove he was just able to cling to a branch of the mango tree. He quickly asked the monkeys to climb over his back and onto the reed in order to escape to the other side.

In this way, eight thousand monkeys climbed over his back one by one and made it to safety.

Unfortunately, there was one bad monkey who hated his leader and wanted to kill him. His name was Devadutta. This mean monkey purposely jumped hard over his poor king's back and broke it, while he himself escaped to the other bank.

*****

King Brahmadutta, who had been awake for awhile, had observed the entire episode. He felt extremely sorry for the monkey king and asked his men to help lower him to the ground. He then had him gently bathed and wrapped in a soft yellow cloth and asked him why he had sacrificed himself for his tribe.

The great monkey answered that as he was their guide and chief, they were his children. So it was his sacred duty to protect them. He had absolutely no regrets, since he had ensured their safety. He also went on to say that the king should always be mindful of his subjects' welfare, even at the cost of his own. Saying this, the monkey king died.

*****

King Brahmadutta had learnt a great deal that day. He ordered his men to organise a funeral fit for a king. He then built a shrine in the monkey king's memory where he offered flowers and lit candles and incense.

On returning to Benares, he built another shrine there and asked his people to pay homage to this great soul. He always remembered the last words of the monkey king and ruled his subjects with wisdom and compassion. The people in his kingdom were eternally grateful to the large-hearted monkey king.

■■

The Treacherous Headman

Once upon a time, King Brahmadutta was ruling in Benares in northern India. He had a clever minister who pleased him very much. To show his appreciation he appointed him headman of a remote border village. His duty was to represent the king and collect the king's taxes from the villagers.

Soon, the headman was completely accepted by the villagers. Since the just King Brahmadutta had sent him, they respected him highly. They came to trust him as much as if he had been born among them. Besides being clever, the headman was also very greedy. Collecting the king's taxes was not enough reward for him. After becoming friendly with a gang of bandits, he cooked up a plan to make himself rich.

The headman told his friends, the robbers, "I will find reasons to lead all the villagers into the jungle. This will be easy for me, since they trust me as one of their own. While I keep them busy in the jungle, you enter the village and rob everything there. Carry everything away before I bring the people home. In return for my help, you must give me half of all the loot!" The bandits agreed, and a date was set.

When the day arrived, the headman assembled all the villagers and led them into the jungle. According to the plan, the bandits entered the unprotected village. They stole everything of value they could find. They also killed all the defenceless village cows, and cooked and ate the meat. At the end of the day, the gang collected all their stolen goods and escaped.

It so happened that on this very day a travelling merchant came to the village to trade his goods. When he saw the bandits he stayed out of sight.

The headman brought all the villagers home in the evening. He ordered them to make a lot of noise by beating drums as they marched towards the village. If the bandits had still been there, they would have heard the villagers coming for sure.

The village people saw that they had been robbed and all their cows were dead and partly eaten. This made them very sad. The travelling merchant appeared and told them, "This treacherous headman has betrayed your trust in him. He must be a partner of the gang of bandits. Only after they left with all your valuables did he lead you home, beating drums as loudly as possible!

"This man pretends to know nothing about what has happened and acts as innocent as a newborn lamb! In truth, it's as if a son did something so shameful that his mother would say — 'I am not his mother. He is not my son. My son is dead!'"

Before long, news of the crime reached the king. He recalled the treacherous headman and punished him according to the law.

■■

The Lazy Student

Once upon a time there was a world famous teacher and holy man in the city of Takshila. He had 500 students training under him. One day these 500 young men went into the forest to gather firewood. One of them came upon a tree with no leaves. He thought, "How lucky I am! This tree must be dead and dry, perfect for firewood. So what's the hurry? I'll take a nap while the others are busy searching in the woods. When it's time to return, it will be easy to climb this tree and break off branches for firewood. So what's the hurry?" He spread his jacket on the ground, lay down on it, and fell fast asleep – snoring loudly.

After a while, all the other students began carrying their bundles of firewood back to Takshila.

On their way they passed the snoring student. They kicked the man to wake him up and said, "Wake up! Wake up! It's time to return to our teacher."

The lazy student woke up suddenly and rubbed his eyes. Still not fully awake, he climbed up the tree. He began breaking off branches and discovered that they were actually still green, not dry at all. While he was breaking one of them, it snapped back and poked him in the eye. So he had to hold his eye with one hand while he finished gathering his bundle of green wood. Then he carried it back to Takshila, running fast to catch up. He was the last one back, and so he threw his bundle on top of the rest.

*****

Meanwhile an invitation to a religious ceremony arrived. It was to be held the next day at a remote village. The holy man told his 500 pupils, "This will be good training for you. You will have to eat an early breakfast tomorrow morning. Then go to the village for the religious service. When you return, bring back my share of the offerings as well as your own."

The students awoke early the next morning. They awakened the college cook and asked her to prepare their breakfast porridge. She went out in the dark to the woodpile. She picked up the top bundle of the lazy man's green wood. She brought it inside and tried to start her cooking fire. But even though she blew and blew on it, she couldn't get the fire going. The wood was too green and damp.

When the sun came up there was still no fire for cooking breakfast. The students said, "It's getting to be too late to go to the village." So off they went to their teacher.

67

The teacher asked them, "Why are you still here? Why haven't you left yet?"

They told him, "A lazy good-for-nothing slept while we all worked. He climbed a tree and poked himself in the eye. He gathered only green wood and threw it on top of the woodpile. The college cook picked this up. Because it was green and damp, she couldn't get the breakfast fire started. And now it's too late to go to the village."

The world-famous teacher said, "A fool who is lazy causes trouble for everyone. When what should be done early is put off until later, it is soon regretted."

■■

The Strong-willed Snake

Once upon a time there was a doctor who was an expert at treating snakebites. One day he was called by the relatives of a man who had been bitten by a poisonous snake.

The doctor told them, "There are two ways of treating this snakebite. One is by giving medicine. The other is by capturing the snake who bit him, and forcing him to suck out his own poison."

The family said, "We would like to find the snake and make him suck the poison out."

After the snake was caught, the doctor asked him, "Did you bite this man?"

"Yes I did," said the snake.

"Well then," said the doctor, "you must suck your own poison out of the wound."

But the strong-willed snake replied, "Take back my own poison? Never! I have never done such a thing and I never will!"

Then the doctor started a wood fire and told the snake, "If you don't suck that poison out, I'll throw you in this fire and burn you up!"

But the snake had made up his mind. He said, "I'd rather die!" And he began moving towards the fire.

In all his years, the snakebite expert had never seen anything like this! He took pity on the courageous snake, and kept him from entering the flames. He then used his medicines and magic spells to remove the poison from the suffering man.

The doctor admired the snake's single-minded determination. He knew that if he used his determination in a wholesome way, he could improve himself. So he taught him the Five Training Steps to avoid unwholesome actions. Then he set him free and said, "Go in peace and harm no one."

■ ■

The Irreplaceable Brother

Once upon a time some bandits robbed a village. Then they escaped into a thick forest. Some men from the village chased them. They surrounded the forest and searched it for the robbers, but they could not find them.

When they came out of the forest they saw three farmers ploughing their field. They immediately captured them and said, "Aha! You bandits are pretending to be innocent farmers interested only in ploughing! Come with us to the king, you thieves!"

They tied the farmers up and took them as prisoners to the king. He locked them in the palace dungeon.

Then a woman began coming to the palace courtyard. For several days she came and cried, as if in mourning. One day the king heard her cries and asked her to come inside. He asked why she was crying. She said, "I have heard that my husband, son and brother are all your prisoners, my lord."

The king had the three men produced before him. Being a generous ruler, he told the woman, "I will give you one of these three. Which one do you choose?"

The woman asked, "Can't you give me all three, my lord?"

The king replied, "No, I cannot."

After considering carefully, she said, "If you will not give me all three, then give me my brother, O King."

The king was surprised by her choice. He said, "You should choose your husband or son. Why would you want your brother instead?"

The smart woman replied, "O my lord, when I go out into the world, a new husband would be easy to find. And then I could easily have another son. A husband or a son is easy to come by in this world. But since my parents are dead, I would never get another brother!"

The king was impressed by the intelligence and reasoning power shown by this simple woman. So he decided to reward her and said, "I return all three to you – your brother, husband and son."

■ ■

The Wrong Drumbeat

Once upon a time there was a drummer living in a small country village. He heard there was going to be a fair in the city of Benares. So he decided to go there and earn some money by playing his drums. He took his son along to accompany him when playing music written for two sets of drums.

The two drummers, father and son, went to the Benares Fair. They were very successful. Everyone liked their drum playing and gave generously to them. When the fair was over they began the trip home to their little village.

On the way they had to go through a dark forest. It was very dangerous because of thieves who robbed travellers. The drummer boy wanted to protect his father and himself from the thieves. So he beat his drums as loudly as he could, without stopping, "The more noise, the better!" he thought.

The drummer man took his son aside. He explained to him that when large groups passed by, especially royal processions, they were in the habit of beating drums. They did this at regular intervals, in a very dignified manner, as if they feared no one. They would beat a drum roll, remain silent, then beat again with a flourish, and so on. He told his son to do likewise, to fool the thieves into thinking there was a powerful lord passing by.

But the boy ignored his father's advice. He thought he knew best. "The more noise, the better!" he thought.

Meanwhile, a gang of thieves heard the boy's drumming. At first they thought it must be a powerful rich man, approaching with heavy security. But then they heard the drumming continue in a wild fashion without stopping. They realised that it sounded frantic, like a frightened little dog barking at a calm big dog.

So they went to investigate and found only the father and son. They beat them up, robbed all their hard-earned money, and escaped into the forest.

■■

The Intelligent Judge

Carrying her child, a woman went to the future Buddha's tank to wash. And having first bathed the child, she put on her upper garment and descended into the water to bathe herself.

Now a *yaksha,* seeing the child, had a craving to eat it. So taking the form of a woman, she drew near, and asked the mother, "Friend, this is a very pretty child. Is it one of yours?" And when told it was, she asked if she might nurse it. And this being allowed, she nursed it a little, and then carried it off.

But when the mother saw this, she ran after her, and cried out, "Where are you taking my child to?" and caught hold of her.

The *yaksha* boldly said, "Where did you get the child from? It is mine!" And so quarrelling, they passed the door of the future Buddha's Judgment Hall.

He heard the noise, sent for them, inquired into the matter, and asked them whether they would abide by his decision. And they agreed. Then he had a line drawn on the ground, and told the *yaksha* to take hold of the child's arms, and the mother to take hold of its legs, and said, "The child shall be hers who drags him over the line."

But as soon as they pulled at him, the mother, seeing how he suffered, grieved as if her heart would break. And letting him go, she stood there weeping.

Then the future Buddha asked the bystanders, "Whose hearts are tender to babes? Those who have borne children, or those who have not?"

And they answered, "Oh sire! The hearts of mothers are tender."

Then he said, "Who, think you, is the mother? She who has the child in her arms, or she who has let go?"

And they answered, "She who has let go is the mother."

So he said, "Then do you all think that the other was the thief?"

Then they answered, "Sire! We cannot tell."

And he said, "Verily, this is a Yaksha, who took the child to eat it. Because her eyes winked not, and were red, and she knew no fear, and had no pity, I knew it."

So saying, he demanded of the thief, "Who are you?"

She said, "Lord! I am a *yaksha*."

Then he asked, "Why did you take away this child?"

She replied, "I thought to eat him, O Lord!"

He rebuked her, saying, "O foolish woman! For your former sins you have been born a *yaksha,* and now you still do sin!" Then he laid a vow upon her to keep the Five Commandments, and let her go.

But the mother of the child exalted the future Buddha, saying, "O my Lord! great physician! May your life be long!" And she went away, with her babe clasped to her bosom.

■■

The Giant Crab

Once, a giant crab lived in a Himalayan lake. He was so large that he caught and killed an elephant to enjoy its flesh. The crab thus created havoc among the elephants and made many flee the lake.

At that time, the queen elephant conceived the Bodhisattva in her womb. Anticipating the possible danger in the lake, the king elephant sent her to a safer place, far from the lake, for delivery.

In course of time, she delivered a baby, who grew up like a purple mountain. He was also wise and brave. Soon, he chose a good and nice female elephant as his companion. By and by, he came to know of the havoc created by the giant crab, who was the cause of the separation from his father. So, he planned to go to the lake and kill the crab.

*****

One day, he marched to the lake with his mates. There, he approached his father and sought his permission and blessing to kill the giant crab. At first the elephant king did not grant him the permission but later allowed him when requested repeatedly.

The Bodhisattva then called upon all his friends to launch an expedition against the crab. His attack was not rash as he collected all relevant information about his enemy, viz., the crab always attacked the last among the retreating animals from the lake. He ordered all the elephants to march to the lake and feed there. When retreating, he deliberately stayed behind all the other elephants. Thus, he was caught by the crab, which held one of his hind legs as a smithy holds the lump of iron between his tongs. The Bodhisattva then pulled up his leg but could not budge an inch. The crab, indeed, was very powerful. The elephant in his peril then trumpeted in a high pitch.

Sensing the danger all the elephants ran helter-skelter. Meanwhile, the crab drew him closer and closer to suck his blood. Seeing the danger, he shouted at his mate not to run away. The female elephant then answered that she would not to leave him in his distress and said:

The question of leaving you does not arise
O noble husband of sixty!
None so dear can be found
On the earth like thee.

She then came near the crab and spoke to him in a sweet voice:

Among all the living crabs in the sea; or
Whether the Ganga or Narmada be;
You are the best and most powerful, I know
Please listen and let my mate go.

Pleased with the female's flattery, the crab loosened his grip with the least suspicion of what the elephant could do. No sooner than the elephant found the grip of the crab loosened, he gave a thunderous cry of elation, which drew all the runaway elephants back. Together, they pulled the crab on the shore and trampled him to mincemeat.

■ ■

The Crafty Jackal

Once the Bodhisattva was born as a tree spirit on the bank of a river. Here, there lived a jackal with his wife. As his wife, the female jackal, was very dear to him, he was always eager to gratify her wishes.

One day, the female jackal expressed her desire to eat the *rohu* fish, and requested the jackal to bring her this. The jackal readily agreed to bring the fish. So, he wandered on the bank of the river to grab an opportunity to find the fish for his dear wife.

Soon, he saw two otters Gambhirachari and Anutirachari standing on the bank in search of a *rohu* fish. Seeing a big fish in the river

Gambhirachari jumped into the river with lightning speed and caught the tail of the fish. But the fish was too big for him and dragged him deeper into the river. Gambhirachari then called upon his friend to help him. Anutirachari then joined his friend to bring the fish on the shore. After some struggle they both finally succeeded in bringing the fish on the shore. There, they killed the fish. But then a dispute began on the question of the division of the fish.

The jackal, who was so far watching the otters, now decided to intervene. He came near them and said that he had been the arbiter for many such cases and could help them by his experience. The otters agreed to his proposed arbitration.

The jackal then said:

Tail to Anutirachari and to
Gambhirachari the head;
The middle to the arbiter,
who must thus be paid.

Next, he advised them not to quarrel and enjoy their shares. Delightfully, he then seized the large portion of the fish and went away.

The two otters were left sitting there with eyes downcast to repent:

Had we not quarrelled we would have enjoyed the fish without fail.

Because we quarrelled the jackal grabs the fish and leaves us head and tail.

The Foolish Jackal

Once there lived a mighty lion in a cave in the Himalayas. One day, after killing and eating a buffalo, when he was on his way back to his cave, he found a jackal prostrating before him. The jackal, in fact, wanted to enjoy the leftovers of the lion.

The lion asked him, "Why do you lie like this, jackal?"

The jackal said, "Sire! I would like to be your servant." The lion accepted his proposal and treated him with affection.

*****

Since that day the lion offered him the leftovers of the animals he killed. Being fed on those the emaciated jackal soon bulged; but so did his pride. Further, he fostered the false idea of having equal power like that of the lion.

So one day, he said to the lion, "O lion! So far I have been fed on your leftovers; but today, I shall offer you my leftovers as I shall kill and eat an elephant."

The lion advised him to refrain from any such act, as he did not belong to the species of lion-like animals to kill a strong elephant.

The haughty and foolish jackal did not listen to the lion. Acting like a lion, he moved out of the cave and uttered the cry of a jackal thrice, as if it was the cry of a mighty lion.

He then looked for an elephant, and saw one at the base of the mountain. He jumped at the large animal from the top of the mountain. But instead of falling on elephant's back, he fell at his feet. Without paying much notice to the existence of the jackal, the elephant lifted his foreleg and placed it on the jackal's head and smashed his skull. Thus the foolish jackal was killed instantly.

The lion witnessed the entire show from the top of the precipice and said:

A reckless and haughty being
Is thus bound to meet his doom.

■ ■

The Hare's Great Sacrifice

Once dwelling in Savatthi, the Buddha extolled the virtue of charity by way of the popular tale that narrates the traditional account of the mark of the hare on the moon.

In one of his previous births the Bodhisattva was born as a hare in Benares. He had three friends – a monkey, a jackal and an otter. Together they resolved to practise charity on the Uposatha day (the day of fast) that was to occur on the following day. In the tradition it was believed that one who stood fast in moral practice and alms giving on that day would earn a great reward.

The next day, the otter brought seven red fish abandoned on the bank of the Ganga River. The jackal wrongfully pilfered a lizard and a pot of milk-curd from somebody's house. The monkey brought a bunch of mangoes. All these three were willing to offer their gifts to some beggar as act of charity. But the hare, when browsing the grass, felt that the grass would not be a good item for alms giving. He, therefore, decided to offer his entire body in charity.

The hare's resolve disturbed Lord Sakka (Indra), the king of the *devas*. To examine the hare's virtue he came down on the earth in the guise of an ascetic and asked the hare for food. The hare was delighted, because this provided him an opportunity to exemplify his highest act of sacrifice, which a mortal could ever perform. So, he asked the ascetic to pile logs of wood and kindle a fire, where he would jump to offer his roasted meat to the latter.

When Sakka caused the heap of burning coals to appear, the hare shook himself thrice lest there were any insects in his fur. Thus, offering his whole body, he fell on the heap of burning twigs.

The fire, however, did not burn him. Impressed with the act, Sakka revealed his identity and applauded the hare's virtue. He said 'O wise hare! Be thy virtue known throughout this whole aeon!" By squeezing the mountain, he then made the sign of the hare on the orb of the moon with its extracted essence.

We thus see the mark of the hare still visible on the moon to tell the saga of the Great Sacrifice.

■■

The Bodhisattva's Penance

Once the Bodhisattva was born in an illustrious family of scholars. He had six younger brothers and one sister. Having mastered the Vedas and the Upavedas (medicinal science, military science, music and architecture) he became famous for his knowledge. Further, he attended to his old and senile parents with great care, and taught his siblings, too.

When his parents died, and the funeral ceremony was over, he made a sudden announcement to renounce worldly life. All his seven brothers and his only sister, too, decided to join him as ascetics. So, they all gave up worldly belongings and headed for the forest. They had two faithful servants, too, one male and one female, who also accompanied them, as they loved their masters.

They went to a forest where there was a large blue lake, which in the daytime displayed the resplendence of expanding lotus-beds; and at nights the exuberance of myriad water lilies exposing their calyxes. All the ascetics decided to stay there and built as many huts as they numbered.

*****

Here, they strictly adhered to their vows and observances and would meet only on every fifth day to listen to the discourse of the Bodhisattva. There lived a *yaksha*, a monkey and an elephant in the same forest, who also joined the audience to listen to the discourse.

The maidservant still served them food. She collected the eatable lotus-stalks from the lake and divided them in eight equal parts on the large lotus-leaves at a clean place on the lakeshore. She would then beat the two pieces of sticks to announce that the food was ready and then walk away silently. Each of the mendicants would come according to seniority and pick up his or her share and go back to their respective huts. Thus, they avoided talking and interacting with each other as an ascetic practice.

*****

Their penance won them great fame. Sakka, the lord of the celestial beings, also heard of their reputation and one day when the food was placed in eight places for the eight ascetics and the announcement of the meal-time was made, he pinched the share of the Bodhisattva to examine the seriousness of his austerity. When the Bodhisattva came and saw his share missing, he quietly went back to his hut to continue with his meditation. Others, however, came and went away with their shares without knowing that the Bodhisattva's share was stolen. Sakka, likewise, stole the Bodhisattva's share consecutively for the following four days.

On the fifth day, when all the ascetics assembled, they noticed that the Bodhisattva looked extremely emaciated and his voice, too, was feeble. After a brief investigation it was discovered that he had to live without any food for five consecutive days as his food was being stolen. All the mendicants then one by one swore that the thief should go back to the household life and become prosperous. Nobody showed any hatred against anybody. The *yaksha*, the monkey and the elephant, who came to listen to the discourse, also prayed for the welfare of the unknown thief.

The prayers and good wishes for the thief made Sakka feel guilty. He then appeared before them and bowed before the Bodhisattva to praise his virtues and to confess his sin.

■ ■

The Haughty Mendicant

Once the Bodhisattva was born into a family of merchants. As per custom, he sold his products in the market. One day, when he was on his usual round of sales, he saw a haughty Brahmin mendicant clad in a leather garment. The mendicant was haughty because he had a very high and false opinion of his spiritual achievements. He thought himself the greatest and had the illusion that every creature in the world was there to honour him.

Soon the merchant saw a ram bowing before the mendicant and about to attack him, as he was wearing a leather garment it had not liked. But the Brahmin, on the contrary, thought that the animal was bowing to honour him.

Witnessing the whole scene from a distance, however, the merchant warned the Brahmin by shouting,

O Brahmin! Don't be rash to trust an animal
As it would make you fall.
If it goes back
It would jump and attack.

But before the Brahmin could hear what the merchant was saying, the ram attacked savagely and knocked him down on the ground, where he lay groaning in pain. And before the merchant could attend to him and apply some first aid, he succumbed to the injury.

■■

Temiya's Pretence

Chanda Devi, the wife of the king of Kashi, had no son. This filled her life with misery. When he saw her grief, the king of the *devas* Sakka decided to help her because she was a virtuous lady. So, he persuaded the Bodhisattva, who was then born in the realm of the Tavatimsa, to prepare for his descent in her womb for the sake of her happiness.

The Bodhisattva then entered the womb of the queen. When he was born, there was heavy rainfall in the city. As he was born wet, he was called *Temiya*.

When Temiya was one month old and lying in his father's lap, he overheard his father's harsh sentence meant for some bandits. This made him remember one of his births when he was the king of Benares and reigned there for twenty years for which he suffered for twenty thousand years in *Ussada Niraya* (a kind of hell).

So he loathed the idea of being a king for the second time. As he was conversant with the deities of the higher world, he received advice from one of them to pretend to be dumb and inactive to avoid the inheritance of the kingdom. He took the advice and accordingly pretended to be dumb and inactive for sixteen years.

*****

Owing to his pretence he was declared unfit as a prince or a future king and was eventually handed over to the royal charioteer Sunanda to be taken to the cemetery where he would be clubbed to death and buried.

When Sunanda was digging the grave to dispose of the dead body, Temiya stealthily sneaked behind him and confided his resolve to him. Impressed, Sunanda then wanted to be an ascetic like him. But Temiya asked him first to inform his whereabouts to the king and his mother, and then become an ascetic.

The king, queen and others soon arrived there. Temiya gave them a sermon to praise the ideals of asceticism. All the people, including the king and the queen, were highly impressed by his sermon and became ascetics. Soon, the fame of Temiya spread all around, which made the citizens of the three kingdoms adjacent to Benares his followers.

■ ■

The Crooked Gambler

Once there lived a rich businessman who was smart and young. He was very fond of gambling. One day when he was on a business tour, he stayed in an inn. There, he was invited for a game of gambling by a veteran gambler who was considered 'unbeatable' in the game. When the game was on, he noticed that his opponent had resorted to foul play by stealthily gobbling up the dice and pretending it was lost. This made the young man lose the game.

The young man, however, did not accept his defeat. He thought of teaching a lesson to the other gambler. So, when he returned home, he smeared a dice with poison and dried it carefully.

*****

The next day, he went to his opponent and challenged him to a fresh round of game. The other gambler again stealthily put the dice into his mouth. But once again, he was detected by the young gambler, who yelled, "Swallow! Swallow! O my dear! Now, you will know what you have swallowed is but poison and not the dice."

The poison was soon at work. The cheat writhed in pain. His eyes rolled and he fainted. As the young man did not have any intention to kill the fellow gambler, he took out some purgative from his bag and made him drink it, which forced him to vomit.

This cured the other fellow. He came back to his senses and never dared to deceive others in the game of dice.

■ ■